GA and SK Etiquette
Guidelines for Telecommunications in the Deaf Community

By Sharon J. Cagle and Keith M. Cagle
Illustrations by Val Nelson-Metlay

Bowling Green Press, Inc.
Bowling Green, Ohio

Published by the Bowling Green Press, Inc., 1435 Rosewood Drive, Bowling Green, OH 43402.

Library of Congress Catalogue Card No. 91-70297.

ISBN No. 0-9614621-7-5.

Printed in the United States of America.

10 9 8 7 6 5 4 3 2

ABOUT THE AUTHORS:

Sharon Jean Cagle

Profoundly deaf since birth, Sharon went to Crotched Mountain School for the Deaf in Greenfield, New Hampshire, through Jr. High School. She graduated in 1977 from Austine School for the Deaf in Brattleboro, Vermont. Her first experience with a TTY was at the Austine School in 1976. She and her husband Keith earned their Bachelors of Social Work from Rochester Institute of Technology (RIT) / National Technical Institute for the Deaf (NTID) in Rochester, New York in 1982. Sharon is completing her Master of Science in Career and Human Resources Development from RIT. Currently, she is also a homemaker and is raising two lovely daughters, Leslie and Kristina. She is also teaching a sign language course at University of Rochester. Keith and Sharon are independent distributors of Matol Botanical International. They reside in Pittsford, New York.

Keith Martin Cagle

Profoundly deaf since birth from Deaf parents, Keith attended and graduated in 1977 from the Oregon State School for the Deaf in Salem, Oregon. His first experience with a teletype was in 1971, when his Deaf family got a Model 15 TTY. Currently, he is a faculty member of the Sign Communication Department at NTID and earned his Master of Science in Educational Administration from the National Leadership Training Program (NLTP) at California State University at Northridge (CSUN) in 1991. He is in demand as a lecturer across the nation on American Sign Language, Deaf & Hearing Cultures, and Non-manual Signals in ASL.

ABOUT THE ILLUSTRATOR:

Val Nelson-Metlay

Profoundly deaf since birth, Val received her education from public schools. She received a Bachelor of Fine Arts from the University of Kansas. She was exposed to sign language in 1976, and to a TTY in 1979. She has worked as a graphic artist at various corporations, including Hallmark and World Book, Inc. She has illustrated the book *The "Real" History of TTY*, written by Bill Graham. She presently works as a freelance illustrator and lives in Rochester with her husband, Don, and son, Monte.

ACKNOWLEDGEMENTS

We wish to deeply thank the following friends and colleagues who have helped us greatly with their opinions, feedback and consultation on the information and illustrations in this handbook.

Stan Bissell, Professor at RIT
Diane Castle, Professor at NTID/RIT
Susan Fischer, Associate Professor at NTID/RIT
Barbara Ray Holcomb, Assistant Professor at NTID/RIT
Thomas Holcomb, Assistant Professor at NTID/RIT
Vicki Hurwitz, Developmental Education Specialist at NTID/RIT
E. Lynn Jacobowitz, Associate Professor at Gallaudet University
Donald Metlay, Research Assistant at University of Rochester
Sharron Metevier Webster, Senior Programmer at NTID/RIT
Danielle Ross, Masters student at McGill University
Al Sonnenstrahl, Executive Director of Telecommunications for the Deaf, Inc.

v

TABLE OF CONTENTS

INTRODUCTION

The teletypewriter, known as a TTY, was mainly used in governmental agencies and businesses until the advent of computers. In 1963, Robert H. Weitbrecht, a deaf man, developed an acoustic coupler that made it possible to connect the telephone to a TTY in order to make phone calls. The coupler and surplus TTYs began to be distributed in the deaf community in the early 1970's.

A telecommunication device is a typewriter-like device that enables deaf people to use the phone. There are two widely used terms for telecommunication devices: TTY and TDD.

The term, TTY, stands for teletypewriter, which often refers to older models used in the late 1960's and 1970's such as Models 15 and 26. The term, TDD, stands for telecommunication devices for the deaf, and refers to much newer and more current electronic devices. The term, TTY, is often preferred among Deaf users for any type of telecommunication device, because it is perceived as more culturally appropriate. Although the term, TDD, was coined by a deaf woman, Betty Broecker, there was a controversy in the *Silent News* about the term, TDD. "For the deaf" implies that only deaf people use TDDs, while, in fact hearing people use these devices also to call deaf people. In this handbook, we will use TTY for both teletypewriter and telecommunication devices used in the deaf community.

Since the rate of transmission in a TTY conversation is only 60 characters per minute, simplicity and speed are crucial. The use of numbers and punctuation marks on many TTYs can be accessed only by pressing the shift "number" key which may sometimes slow the rate of communication down. The transmission is "half duplex" which means that only one person can "talk" at a time.

The purpose of this handbook is to assist both hearing and deaf callers to become more aware of suggested etiquette for using the TTY. This can reduce potential misunderstandings, since there are some cultural differences between the Deaf and Hearing Worlds. This will be explained by examples comparing telephone behavior in the Hearing Culture (among hearing people) with the Deaf Culture (among deaf people).

These guidelines are based on interviews and surveys conducted with deaf people from numerous states in America and on the results of consulting with the people listed earlier in the acknowledgement.

GA and SK Etiquette:

Guidelines for Telecommunications
in the Deaf Community

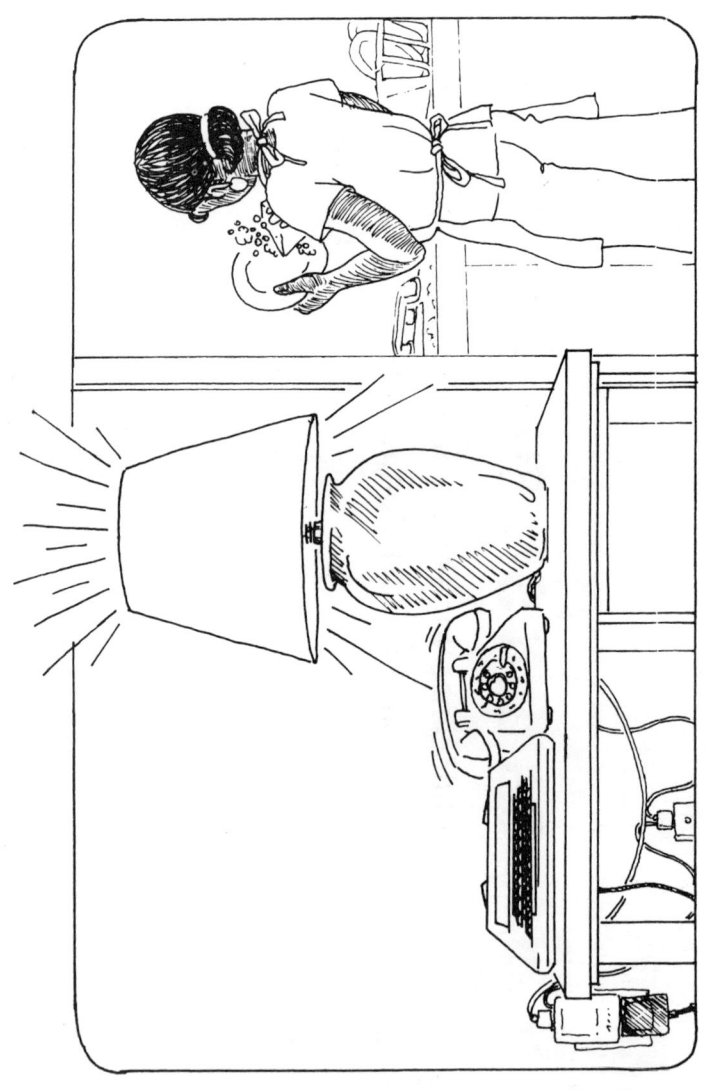

5, 10 or 20 RINGS

In the hearing culture, it is common for a caller to allow 3 to 6 rings before hanging up after deciding no one is home. However, in the deaf culture, the deaf caller generally allows 10 or more rings before hanging up. The difference is due to the fact that deaf people can't hear the phone's ringing, which can penetrate through the walls and reach the ears. Instead, a special flashing light system alerts deaf people to the telephone ringing. Light cannot penetrate through walls; thus, it takes longer to get a deaf person's attention. A deaf person can easily miss the light if the room is bright or his/her back is to the light. Also, it is common for hearing people to have more telephones installed than deaf people, because each TTY costs much more than a telephone.

The caller should be sensitive to hearing people who may live with a deaf person, e.g., spouse, child(ren), roommate, office mate or apartment neighbor, by allowing only six to eight rings. Continuous ringing may be irritating to them. Similarly, hearing people have to be aware that they need to wait longer to allow a deaf person on the other end to "see" the "ringing" (flashing light).

4

VOICE OR TTY?

If you are a hearing person and have a TTY, you normally answer the phone by voice. If you hear nothing or perhaps a series of "beeps," place the phone on the TTY coupler immediately and answer the call.

When placing the phone on the TTY coupler, be sure to look for an arrow showing the correct direction of the handset. If it is placed wrong, the TTY will not function properly.

If you are a deaf person calling a hearing person, it is helpful to tap keys on the TTY several times to let the hearing person know it is a TTY call. Some newer TTY's have a tape recording that explains "Hearing impaired caller; please use TDD."

Some hearing people assume that a TTY call is a crank call and hang up. This can be annoying to people who try to call on the TTY.

Example of "hanging up" without checking if it is a TTY call:

Voice: "hello" "hello"; then hang up.

Example of checking to see if it's a TTY call.

Voice: "hello" "hello"; then try to use TTY and type "HELLO THIS IS . . . ." to see if it is a TTY call.

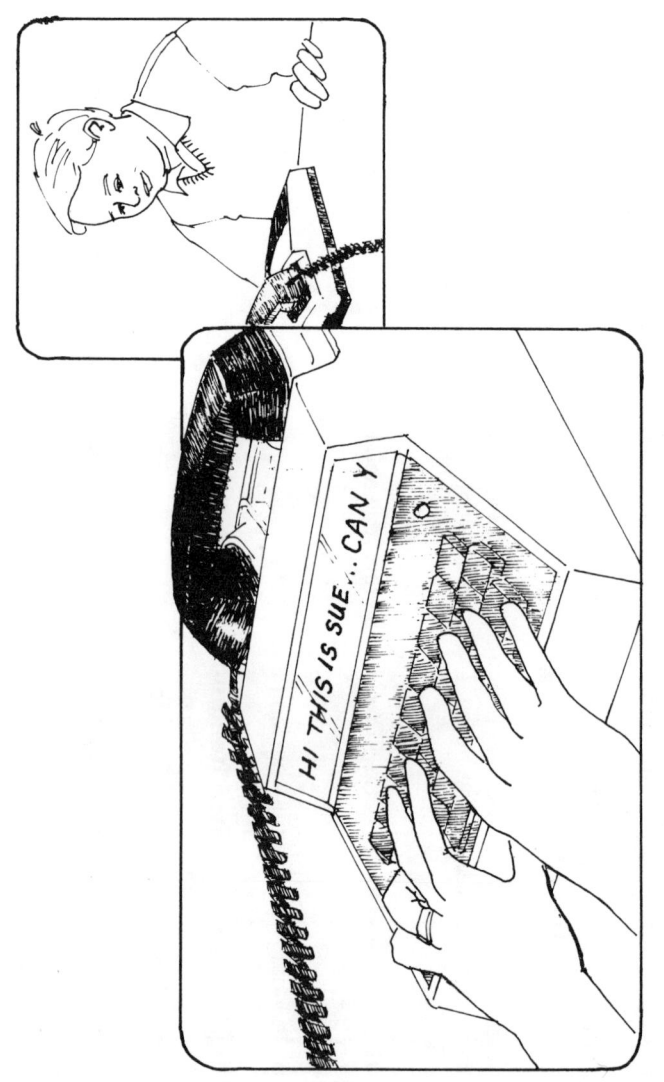

HELLO THIS IS . . . .

It is common for hearing callers to not give their names on the phone, because they often can recognize and identify each others' voices. However, deaf callers cannot do this; therefore, it is helpful and polite to mention your name immediately when you answer a TTY call.

Example of an impolite answering:
"HELLO GA"

or

"GA"

Example of an ideal TTY answering:

"HELLO THIS IS MARY GA"

7

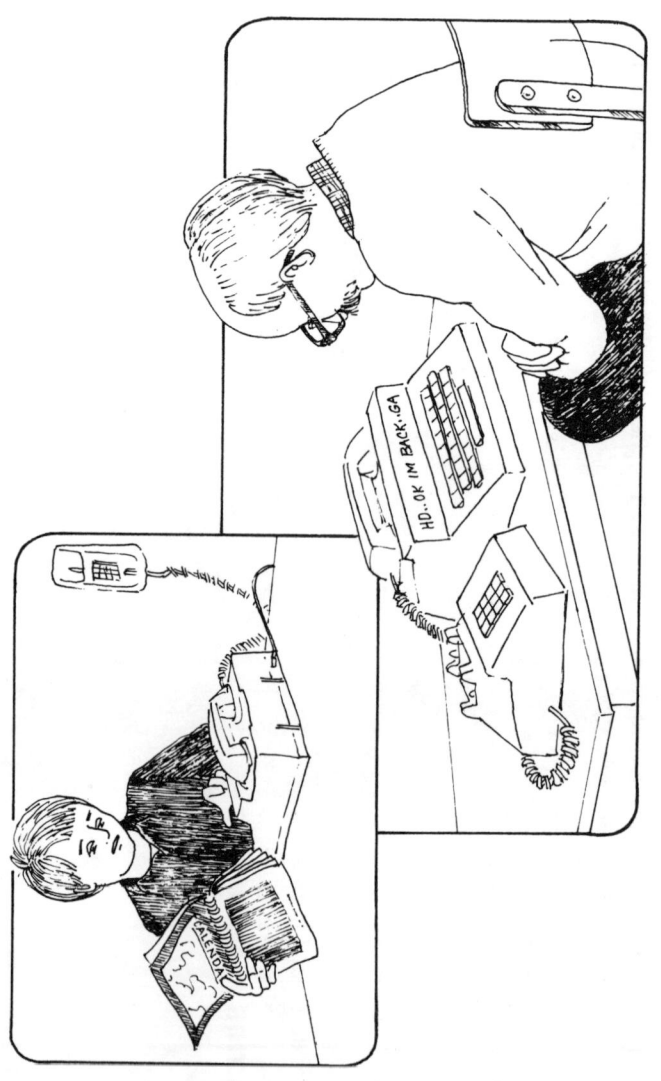

GA HD SK

At the end of your turn during a conversation, you should type **"GA"** as a signal for the person on the other end to go ahead and begin typing. As only one person can "talk" at a time **"GA"** is very important for successful turn taking.

"HD" is a signal to inform that the call is being put on HOLD for a temporary period of time.

When you both are finished with the call, you should type **"SK"** as a signal for "signing off" or "stop keying". This allows both of you to hang up.

Example of not using signals:

"THIS IS JULIE"

Example of using signals:

"THIS IS JULIE GA"

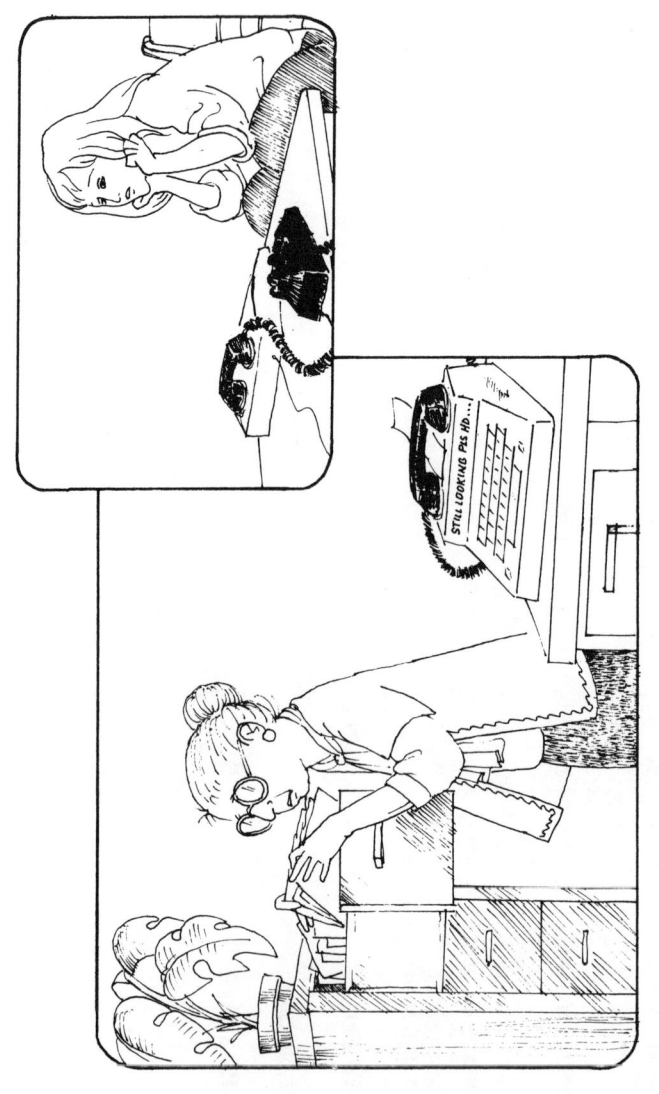

HOLD HOLD HOLD

When you are putting the person on the other end on HOLD for a long time, it is helpful to let the person know that you are still there by typing messages such as **"HD I AM CHECKING," "HD SHE IS COMING,"** or **"HD AGAIN PLEASE I AM STILL LOOKING"** rather than leaving the person on hold for a long time without any word from you. Sometimes the person will hang up on you, because s/he has no idea of what is going on at the other end, or may think the line was disconnected, and hang up.

If it is a long distance call or is during a busy time, you can type something like **"HD OR SHOULD I CALL YOU BACK Q"** or **"PLEASE CALL BACK GA"**

Example of an inappropriate HD:

"PLS HD" (leave it on hold for a very long time)

Example of an appropriate HD:

"PLS HD" (if you need to be on hold longer, inform the other end), **"STILL CHECKING PLS HD"**

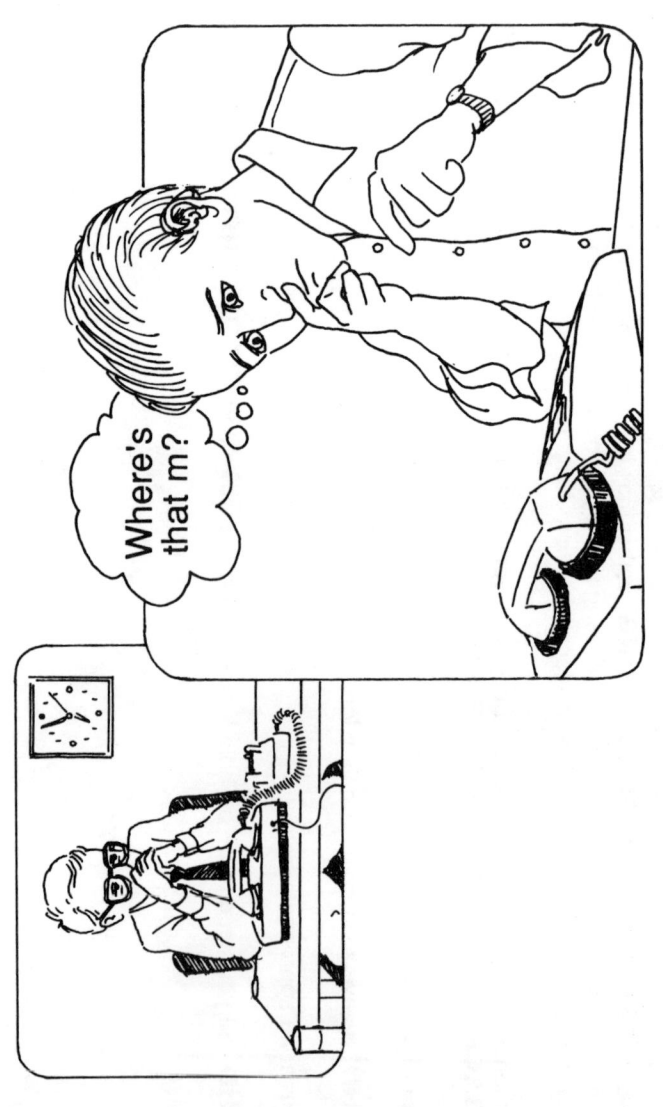

H I   M Y   N A . . . . . (slow typist)

Generally, deaf people prefer to keep their conversation SHORT with people who type SLOWLY. Some people may not have good typing skills, and use their index finger to find the word. This takes much longer than a person with better typing skills.

To speed up the conversation, TTY typing may not need to include punctuation marks (. , : ;) that do not contribute to the content of the message. Punctuation marks often omitted because it is necessary to press two keys to produce them, which is time-consuming. Some letters can be substituted for punctuation marks (e.g., **Q** for ?). Abbreviations are fine as long as they are clear. Known abbreviations used on the TTY are listed on page 52. Other commonly used abbreviations are some English abbreviations for the names of the months and days (e.g., **DEC** for December and **TUES** for Tuesday).

To beginner typists, to change from letters to numbers can be confusing. It is okay to spell out numbers.

Example of a slow conversation:

"COULD YOU READ ME?   I WANT TO THANK YOU FOR THE MESSAGE . . . . . ."

Example of "speeding up" of the conversation:

"CD U RD ME?   I WANT TO TK U FOR MSG. . . . ."

13

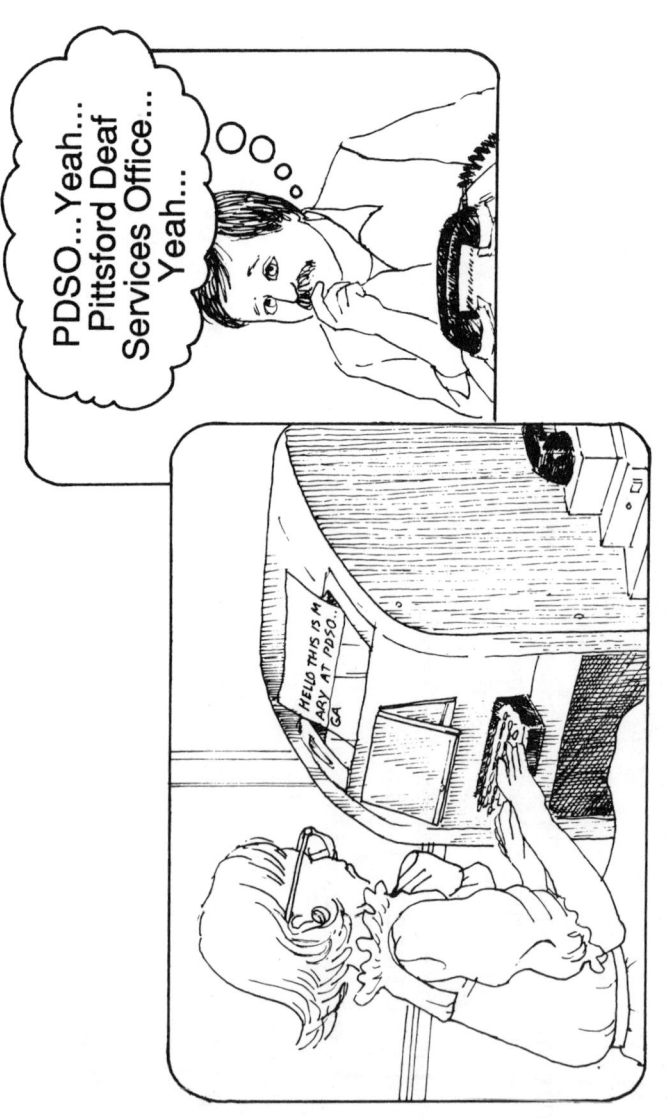

14

K.I.S.S.

...... Yet, Keep your <u>I</u>ntroduction <u>S</u>hort and <u>S</u>weet!

When you answer a TTY call, long introductions can be time consuming and annoying for some busy deaf callers, because they usually know to whom and where they are making the calls. They are also often familiar with the abbreviations of common names in the local deaf community. However, if a national call is made, it is better to use full names. In the deaf culture, deaf people usually make their points and messages quickly and briefly at the beginning of the conversation.

An example of a long introduction is

"GOOD AFTERNOON THIS IS PITTSFORD DEAF SERVICES OFFICE THIS IS MARY DOE SPEAK-ING HOW MAY I HELP YOU Q GA"

An ideal example of KISS is:

"HELLO THIS IS MARY AT PDSO GA"

or

"HELLO THIS IS MARY AT PITTSFORD DEAF SERVICES GA"

15

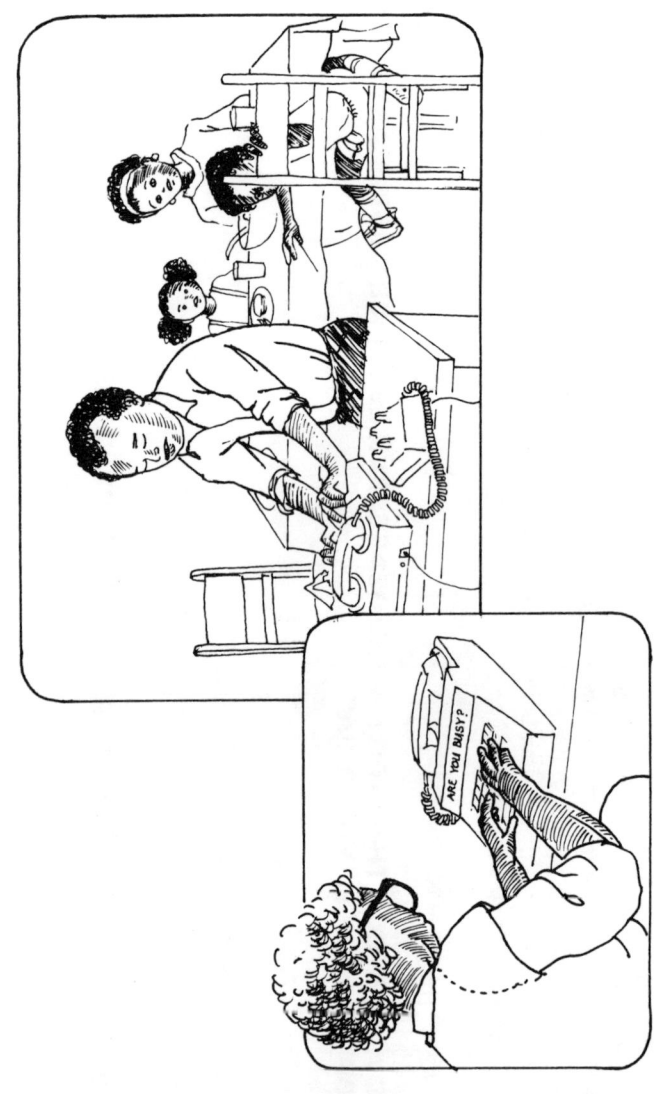

HAVE A MINUTE FOR ME???

As with voice calls, when you are planning to have a long conversation on the TTY, it is polite to ask the person immediately if she or he is busy or is available for a long conversation. You may type messages such as

"HELLO JOE THIS IS JILL DO YOU HAVE SEVERAL MIN Q I WANT TO TALK ABOUT MEETING THIS SATURDAY GA"

Example of a long conversation without asking first:

Caller A: **"HELLO THIS IS BOB GA"**

Caller B: **"HELLO THIS IS NATHAN GUESS WHO I SAW AT THE PARTY I SAW SUSAN AND WE CHAT FOR THREE HRS WE TALKED ABOUT** (blah blah blah)**"**

Example of a long conversation with asking first:

Caller A: **"HELLO THIS IS BOB GA"**

Caller B: **"HELLO THIS IS NATHAN IS IT GOOD TIME TO TALK WITH YOU ABOUT PARTY . . . QQ GA"**

17

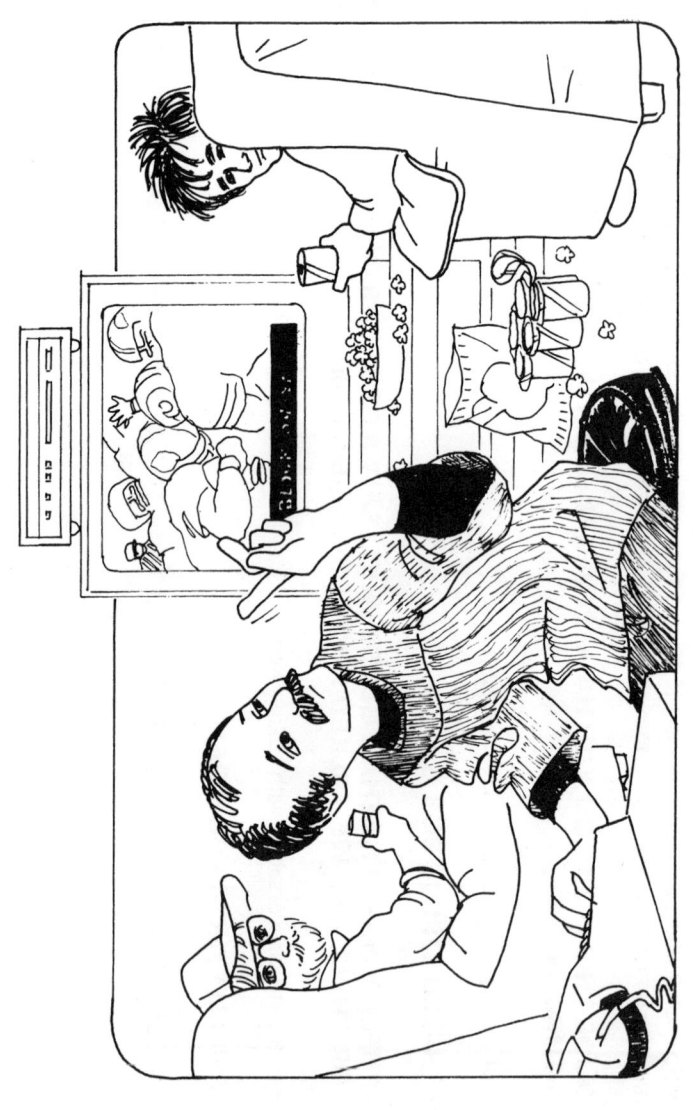

WHO WHO WHO?

It is helpful and courteous when a TTY call interrupts your conversation with a person who is in the room to let that person know who is calling you. You may say something like, "Oh, this is Mary," "one of my students, excuse me," or "long distance from my friend" rather than leaving her/him feeling isolated for a while.

One difference between voice calls and TTY communication is that with voice, a hearing person in the same room can overhear part of the conversation. Most of the time, in a TTY conversation, another person in the room cannot "oversee" a conversation unless she or he is granted permission (see page 27).

Example of not letting others know:

"Excuse me, I am on the phone" (The other person may wonder if he is being talked about.)

Example of courteously letting others know:

"Excuse me, it is one of my students on the phone."

19

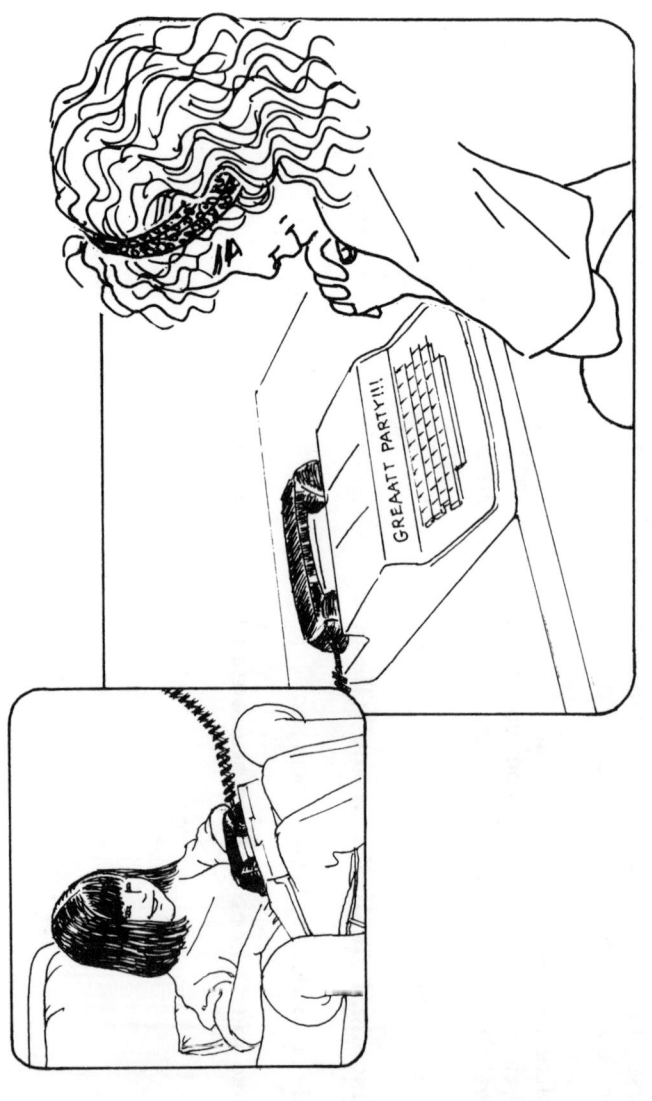

SHOWING FEELINGS ON THE TTY

During a conversation on the TTY, it can be difficult to sense what the person on the other end is feeling, because their facial expression or tone of voice are not accessible.

One way to show your emotion is to add your feelings on the machine by typing this such as

"I AM LAUGHING. . ." "OHHHHH" "HA HA HA" "GREATTT IDEA!!!!"
"THANKS A MILLION" "GRRR" "BOO" or **"SMILE."**

Examples of no feelings on TTY:

"I HAD A GOOD TIME LAST NIGHT THANK YOU GA"

Example of added feelings:

"WWOWWWW I HAD SO MUCH FUN GRRREEATTT!!! LET'S DO IT AGAIN!!!"

WHAT LANGUAGE? XLMN$#%93jma.

It is not polite to interrupt the conversation until the person on the other end completes typing the message **"GA"** for "Go ahead." An exception is when there is a garbled message on your TTY or if you are receiving only numbers. Then it may be necessary to interrupt by typing **"HOLD HOLD HOLD"** or **"XX STOP PLS XX STOP PLEASE"** or **"HEY HEY"**; then wait for a little while to see if the other person has stopped typing. If it is hard to interrupt the conversation, you may have to wait until the other person stops typing. Then you can say **"I READ U IN NBRS SORRY YOUR MESSAGE WAS GARBLED PLS TYPE AFTER I MEET U AT QQ"** or **"PLS REPEAT."** Other technical solutions to clear up the message are to turn your device off and on quickly or press the **"K"** key. Sometimes there is a bad telephone connection that will affect TTY transmission; then the solution is to hang up and dial the number again.

Example of an impolite interruption:

Caller A: **"I WANT TO KNOW HOW TO DO ASSIGNMENT. . ."** (Interrupted)

Caller B: (Interrupting).. **"YES I CAN HELP YOU ON HOW TO DO ASSIGNMENT FOR OUR CLASS TONIGHT GA"**

Example of a proper interruption:

Caller A: **"SXKTH 56HM OXYD. . ."**

Caller B: **"STOP HOLD CANT READ YOU HD GA"**

23

OOOOOOPPPSSS!!!

When you are typing a message with errors, it is not always necessary to use the BACKSPACE to correct misspelling. If you make a mistake with a word or a sentence, it is better if you just type **"XXX"** immediately as a symbol for ignoring the preceding letter, word, sentence or concept. Then you can proceed with a new letter, word, sentence or concept. For example, if you type an incorrect word, don't type like this **"FASTIN CINATING"**; it is better to retype the whole word: **"FASTIN XX FASCINATING."**

Simply typing mistakes or missed letters may sometimes be acceptable, and they may not need to be corrected. For example, in the sentences, **"I LIKE TO READ YOUR PAPPERS"** or **"I LOVE TO EAT AN APLE PIE"** the errors may be acceptable.

The reasons for limiting the use of backspace are several. (1) the other person's TTY may be an older model which does not have the backspace feature and therefore, time and effort to backspace will be wasted. Typing **"XX"** often works better. (2) It is also time-consuming to watch people correct minor errors on the TTY when the reader has already understood what the typist was trying to say. Otherwise, sometimes the person on the other end may ask for clarification.

It is helpful when the other end types phone numbers or addresses, to repeat what you have read, to be sure you got it right. Sometimes the TTY garbles and mixes up the information you need.

Example of acceptable errors: **"I LIKE TO READ YOUR PAPPERS"**

Example of corrected error: **"I LOKE XX LIKE TO READ YOUR PAPERS"**

25

NOSY EYES???

It is not polite to look over someone's shoulder to read her/his TTY conversation, unless you are granted permission. If a person who has never seen a TTY before is curious and would like to watch your conversation, then you should alert the person at the other end and that your TTY conversation is being observed.

Example of an inappropriate behavior:

Looks over someone's shoulder when they are typing on the TTY.

Example of an appropriate approach to ask someone if you could watch:

A friend sees a person typing on the TTY and asks her if it is okay that she observes how the TTY works. She may reply, "Fine", and then type **"HI MY FRIEND HAS NEVER SEEN TTY BEFORE COULD WE SHOW HER FOR A FEW MIN Q GA"**

Whew! Will talk about Beth's surprise party another time.

... BETH IS HERE ...

TO DO's FOR BETH'S PARTY

28

BETH IS READING US.....

If the person on the phone grants someone in the room permission to look over her shoulder to read the TTY conversation, it is courteous to let the person at other end know who else is reading the conversation.

Example of "Beth is reading us" with the other end not knowing:

Caller B: **"WE ARE HAVING BIRTHDAY PARTY FOR BETH THIS FRIDAY GA"**
Caller A: **"GEE   BETH IS READING US"**
Caller B: **"OOOOOPPPSS"**

This can cause an embarrassing situation for both ends.

Ideal example of letting the other end know "Beth is reading us":

Caller A: **"HI THIS IS PATTI MY FRIEND BETH IS WITH ME GA"**
Caller B: **"HI THIS IS KATHY HOW ARE U BOTH GA"** (with relief because she knows not to say what she doesn't want anyone other than Patti to know).

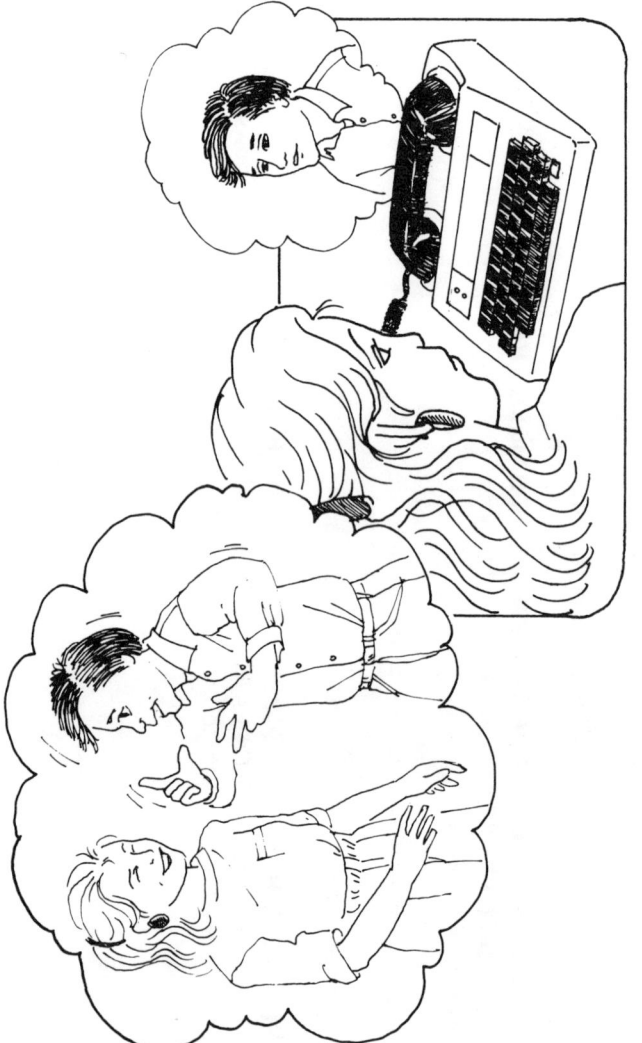

IS THAT JOE??? CAN'T BE!

It is important to understand the impact of the differences between face-to-face and TTY conversations. They may often look different due to the different languages and modalities being used.

It is common for a deaf person to use American Sign Language or another communication mode very fluently in face-to-face conversation, but to not be easily understood on the TTY. This is due to his/her use of a different language: English. Often the typed information on the TTY is not communicated exactly as it would be in ASL due to the absence of facial expression and limitations in terms of showing feeling on the TTY.

Also, It is common for hearing callers with limited signing skills to find deaf people talking more to them on a TTY than during face-to face conversation.

31

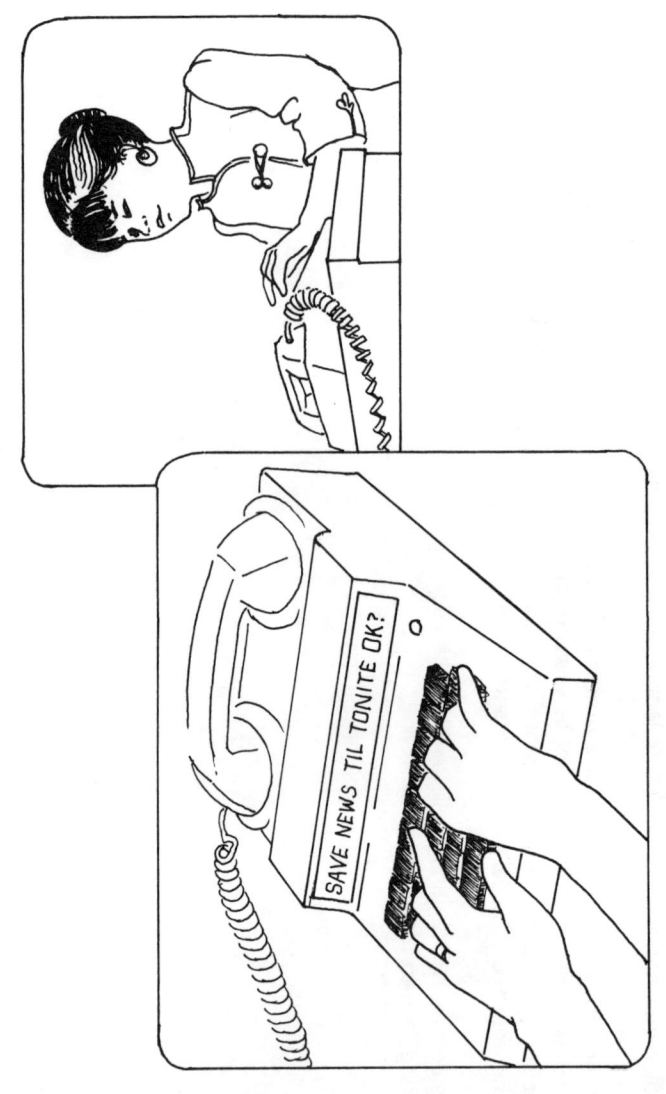

SAVE NEWS UNTIL SEE IN PERSON???

Typing on the TTY can take at least four to five times longer (depending on the person's typing skills) than a typical voice conversation on the phone. Therefore, most deaf people prefer to shorten their local calls enough to complete business such as making arrangements to meet, making any cancellations, delivering an important message or gathering information. More detailed conversations are usually reserved for face-to-face meetings. This is because many deaf people, if they live close, prefer to see each other in person so that they can communicate more quickly by signing. An exception is if the call is long distance. Then it may be longer.

Example of too long:

"I WANT TO LET YOU KNOW THERE IS MTG TMW   I HAD HARD TIME GETTING EVERYONE TO GET TOGETHER   FOR EXAMPLE I CALLED MARK LAST NIGHT   HE HAD A CONFLICT WITH HIS CLASS   THEN I CALLED GEORGIA   (blah blah blah). . ."

Example of saving news until personal contact:

"JUST A SHORT CALL TO LET U KNOW THERES MTG TMW AT 8 PM AT DEAF CLUB   I WILL EXPLAIN MORE TMW ABOUT HARD TIME TO GET EVERYONE GA"

33

AWWW. . . . PHONE RINGING   WHY   NOW??

Generally, many Deaf people prefer not to get calls after 8:00 or 9:00 p.m. when there are good captioned programs on television. However if the call is important, an emergency or very urgent, you may make the call.

Often hearing people have phones with long cords which they can bring to the living or family room to watch television. They can then have a conversation on the phone and watch T.V. at the same time. Deaf people often have their TTYs in their halls, kitchens or dens and therefore can't bring them to the family or living rooms. It is difficult for TTY callers to pay attention to two separate events visually.

It is helpful to become familiar with your friends' typical favorite TV programs or busy times, such as supper time, in order to avoid irritating them.

If you know the other person has an answering machine, it may be all right to call and leave a message without interrupting.

An example of irritating late calls:

"I WENT TO THE PARTY AND (blah blah). . . . . ."

Ideal example of late calls:

"SORRY TO CALL YOU LATE   IT IS IMPORTANT   OK WITH YOU Q GA"

35

PLS CALL BACK BYE SK

If, during a conversation, you need to close and hang up fast for some reason such as an emergency or because your attention is needed urgently, you may type a fast closing such as **"WILL CALL BACK GA TO SK"** or **"MY BOSS IS HERE WITH ME NOW WILL CALL BACK GA TO SK"** or **"WILL CALL BACK CUZ BABY IS CRYING GA TO SK"** or **"JIM JUST CAME IN AND NEEDS ME I WILL CALL BACK BYE GA TO SK."**

If you answer the phone but you have to go to a meeting immediately, you may type a fast message and closing such as **"PLEASE EXCUSE ME I HAVE TO GO TO A MEETING NOW   PLS CALL BACK AT 4:00 PM   OK   Q   THANKS   BYE   GA TO SK."**

Example of an inappropriate quick closing:

Caller A: **"BYE GA TO SK"**
Caller B: **"I AM NOT FINISH GA"** (Puzzled)
Caller A: **"MUST GO SKSK"**

Example of an appropriate quick closing:

Caller A: **"HAVE TO GO NOW CUZ BABY CRYING   WILL CALL BACK OK Q GA TO SK"**
Caller B: **"OK   BYE   SK"**

ONE OR MANY SKs?

Typically, two, or sometimes three "SKs" at the end of the conversation are adequate. More than four SKs can appear rude to the person on the other end. He may interpret many SKs as a signal that you want to get away quickly or you are angry.

Example of inappropriate too many SK's

Caller A: **"HAVE A GOOD DAY   SEE YOU SOON GA TO SK"**
Caller B: **"TKS   YOU HAVE A NICE DAY TOO BYE SKSKSKSKSKSKSK"**
Caller A: (PUZZLED)

Example of one or two appropriate SK's:

Caller A: **"HAVE A GOOD DAY   SEE YOU SOON GA OR SK"**
Caller B: **"TKS   YOU HAVE A NICE DAY TOO BYE GA TO SK"**
Caller A: **"BYE SK SK"**
Caller B: **"SK"**

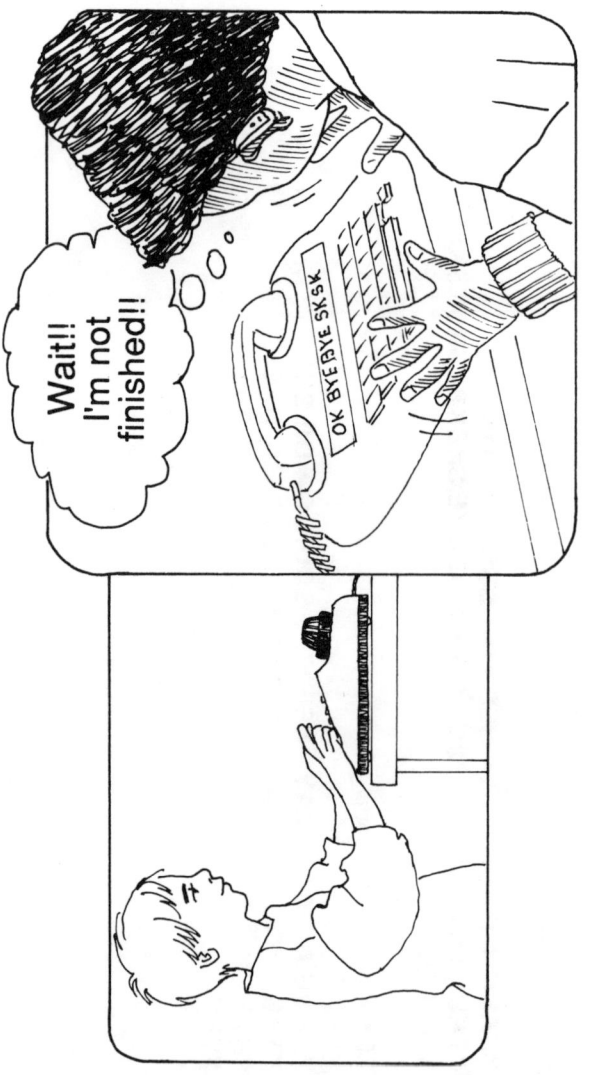

PING PONG CLOSING

Before you finish up your conversation, it is polite to type **"GA OR SK"** or **"GA TO SK"** to allow the person on the other end to close the conversation and make sure both parties have said everything they wanted to.

Example of an inappropriate closing:

Caller A: **"HAVE A NICE DAY   GA OR SK"**
Caller B: **"SKSK"**

Example of an ideal closing:

Caller A: **"HAVE A NICE DAY   SEE U TMW GA OR SK"**
Caller B: **"LOOK FORWARD TO SEE U TMW   TAKE CARE GA TO SK"**
Caller A: **"BYE BYE SK"**
Caller B: **"SKSK"**

41

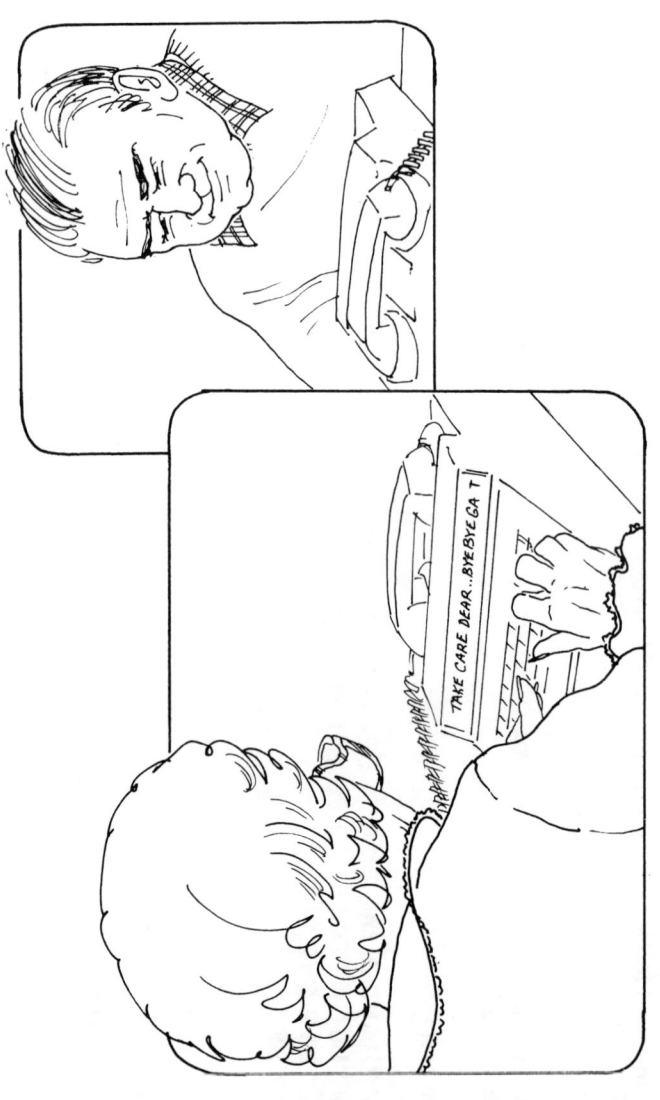

GRACEFUL GOODBYE

It is polite to add some formal kind of leave taking at the end of a conversation before you hang up. You may type something like **"HAVE A NICE DAY BYE BYE..."** or **"SEE YOU LATER..."** or **"THANKS FOR CALLING BYE BYE..."** before you type **"SK SK."**

If you just type **"SK SK"** quickly, you will appear rude. In the deaf culture, people usually have longer greetings and leave taking rituals than in the hearing culture. For business calls, or calls that are not personal calls, a short goodbye is considered to be graceful and friendly. For personal calls, the graceful goodbye tends to be longer.

Example of a possible rude goodbye:

Caller A: **"HAVE A NICE DAY BYE GA TO SK"**
Caller B: **"SKSK"**

Example of an ideal polite goodbye:

Caller A: **"HAVE A NICE DAY BYE GA TO SK"**
Caller B: **"THANK YOU... YOU HAVE A NICE DAY TOO... SEE U SOON BYE BYE SK"**

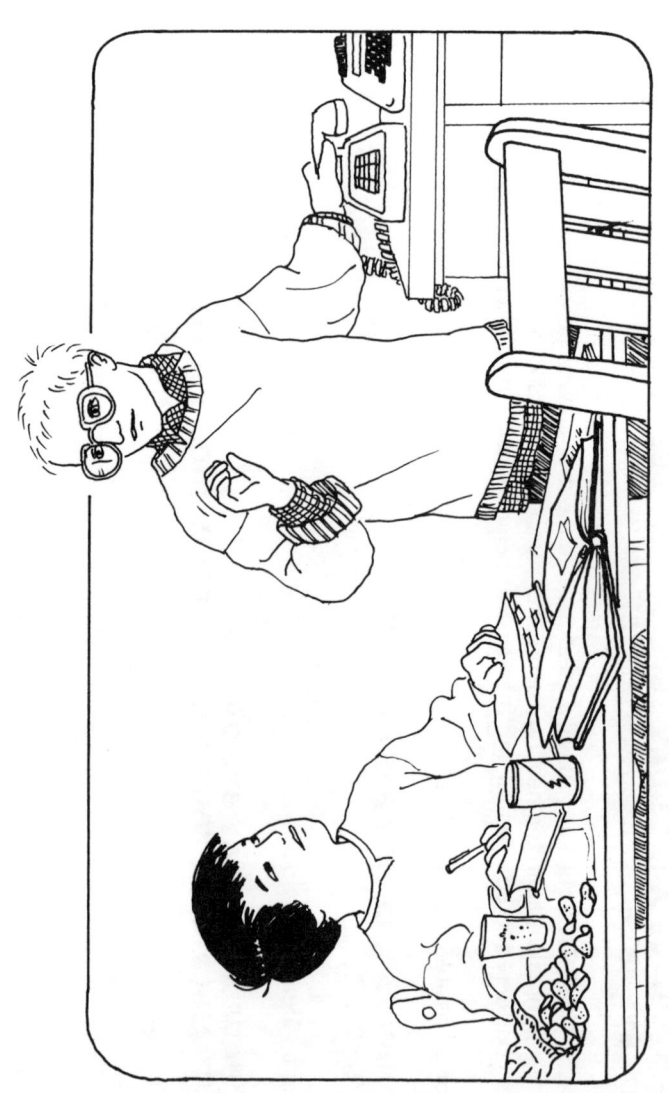

THAT WAS. . . .

It is common during and especially after a TTY conversation for deaf people to share a brief summary of the conversation with others in the room. Most of the time they will say who they were talking with, for example: "Oh, it was Mary talking about the Tupperware party next week." Perhaps this kind of information-sharing occurs more in the deaf culture than in the hearing culture because acoustic information is easily accessible to hearing people. Much information concerning phone calls for hearing people can be overheard. This, of course, is not the case for TTY conversations.

Example of not sharing information:

(Walking around silently after finishing the conversation on TTY.)

Example of sharing information:

"That was my mother. She informed me of my new nephew born today."

45

SAVE TTY PAPER PRINTOUT?

Some TTY models have paper printouts. Most TTY users would enjoy rereading the TTY conversations.

Some agencies or offices occasionally keep the TTY conversation output in the client or patient's files. It may be an unethical violation of privacy to keep TTY output if the deaf client is not aware of this practice. If some information is important and needed, such as an address, a date, or a telephone number, it can be copied on another piece of paper and placed in the file. The TTY output can, then, be destroyed. Agencies should keep in mind that when the client or patient is a hearing person, a recording of their telephone conversations is not kept in their files without their knowledge and consent.

47

SUMMARY OF TIPS

5, 10 or 20 rings: When calling a deaf person, it is appropriate to allow the phone to ring about 10 times.

Voice or TTY: Make an extra effort to determine whether the caller is using a TTY by checking with a TTY before hanging up.

GA HD SK: "GA" means GO AHEAD; **"HD"** means HOLD; **"SK"** means STOP KEYING so as to close the conversation.

HOLD HOLD HOLD: It is considered polite to type **"HOLD HOLD"** before walking away from the TTY temporarily.

HELLO THIS IS: It is considered polite to introduce your name immediately on the TTY.

HI MY NA. . . (slow typist): Be considerate of the person on the other end of the phone line when you are typing slowly. (Using abbreviations will be helpful.

K.I.S.S.: Keep your introduction short and sweet.

HAVE A MINUTE FOR ME ? ? ?: When you wish to speak longer than usual with someone, be considerate, and ask if they have time to talk with you for a quite long time.

WHO WHO WHO?: It is considered normal for a deaf caller to tell family members or friends who are in the same room who is on the phone.

Showing Feelings on the TTY: You may add several extra identical letters at the end of a word and tune-up words to express emotions on a TTY.

What Language???: If the message is garbled on the TTY, you may press the **"K"** key, turn the TTY off and on, type **"HOLD PLS STOP"** repeatedly, or wait until the other person stops and types **"GA."**

OOOOPPSS!: You may type **"XXX"** or ignore the mistake if it is not a major error. Some old TTY's can't backspace.

Nosy Eyes???: If you wish to read another person's conversation on a TTY, it is considered more polite if you request permission.

BETH IS READING US: It is considered more polite to let the person on the other end of the phone know that someone is reading the conversation.

Is that Joe? Can't Be!: Sometimes you may find that the person's TTY communications (style, grammar, and vocabulary) and in-person communications are very different.

Save News Until see in Person???: It is common for deaf persons making local calls to keep messages short on the TTY and say more in person.

AWWW. . . .Phone ringing; Why Now?: Be considerate of what time you are calling a person.

PLS CALL BACK BYE SK: If for any reason it is urgent for someone to stop and hang up, please always let the other person know.

One or Many SKs?: One or two SKs is considered adequate to close the conversation. Many SKs may be considered rude.

Ping Pong Closing: It is considered polite to type **"GA OR SK"** to let the other person know you are ready to close, rather than to type **"SK"** immediately.

Graceful Good-Bye: It is normal for a person to type a longer "good-bye" greeting before closing and hanging up.

"That was....": It is not uncommon for someone to summarize a TTY conversation for family or friends in the same room.

Save TTY Paper Printout?: It is considered more polite to request a person's permission if you wish to keep the TTY paper after the conversation is over.

BIBLIOGRAPHY

Bienvenu, M. J., & Colonomos, B. (1985). *An introduction to American culture: Rules of social interaction* (Videotape). Silver Spring, MD: Sign Media.

Castle, D. L. (1984). *Telephone training for hearing impaired person: Amplified telephones, TDDs, codes.* (2nd ed.). Rochester, NY: National Technical Institute for the Deaf.

Jacobowitz, E. L. (1988). TTY etiquette. *Silent News*, May.

Nash, J. E., & Nash, A. (1982). Typing on the phone: How the deaf accomplish TTY conversations. *Sign Language Studies, 36,* 193–216.

So you now have a telecommunications device for the deaf. (1986). Rockville, MD: National Association for Hearing and Speech Action.

ABBREVIATIONS

It is common for deaf people to use many of abbreviations in their TTY conversations. This is used to shorten the length of time spent on the TTY. Common abbreviations are as follows:

ABT	About
AM	Morning
ANS	Answer
BEC, CUZ	Because
CA	Communication Assistant (Relay Operator)
CD, CU	Could
CN	Can
CUL	See you later
GA	Go Ahead
GOVT	Government
HAND	Have a nice day
HD, HLD	Hold
INFO	Information
ILY	I love you
KIT	Keep in touch
LTR	Letter
LV	Leave
MIN	Minute
MSG	Message
MTG	Meeting

N	And
NBR	Number
NITE	Night
NP	No problem
NOYB	None of your business
OK	Okay
OIC	Oh I see
OPR	Operator
OXOX	Hugs and kisses
PLS	Please
PM	Afternoon, evening
Q, QQ, ?	Question mark
R	Are
RD	Read
REC	Receive
SHD	Should
SK	Stop keying
THNK, TKS, THX	Thanks
THRU	Through
TY	Thank you
TMW, TMR	Tomorrow
U	You
UR	Your
WD, WUD	Would
XX	Errors

HELPFUL INFORMATION:

TELECOMMUNICATIONS FOR THE DEAF, INC. (T.D.I.) founded in 1968, publishes an international telephone directory for TDD users, which contains over 20,000 telephone listings for TTY/TDD's. The directory divides the listings into states and countries under the categories of resident, vocational services, travel & lodging services, social organizations, religious organizations, government, legal services, interpreting services, insurance & financial services, hearing & speech services, education, schools and colleges, business and emergency. The directory has listings of answering, relay, and hot line services, TDD numbers, and Toll free 800 numbers for Airlines, federal agencies, etc. For more information, or to obtain the directory, write to TDI, 8719 Colesville Rd., Suite 300, Silver Spring, MD 20910. They also have a 30 minutes videotape for hearing people showing how to use a TTY, "Using your TTY/TTD," which is useful, convenient and time effective for places where there are high turnovers such as corporations, hospitals, emergency centers, schools, to name a few.

An A.T.T. TTY Operator, 1-800-855-1155: will answer any questions, or assist you concerning your AT&T bill, AT&T card, Reach Out America, Opportunity Calling, AT&T long distance certificates, making collect or person to person calls or calls from motels or hotels. They will also assist you in finding telephone numbers which are not in your book. The AT&T Special Needs Center will also be of assistance.

RELAY SERVICES: These services assist hearing and deaf person by communicating simultaneously with each party. An operator voices the typed message from the deaf person to the hearing person and vice versa. Relay services are listed in the international telephone directory for TDD users.

54